EXPLORE ABC FUN

An Assembled Alphabet Adventure

written and illustrated by

CATHY ROWE

RYN
FOX
INK

Cover design and book layout by
Claire Flint Last at Luminare Press
www.LuminarePress.com

Ryn Fox Ink
923 Hazelwood Dr.
Oregon City, OR 97045
www.RynFoxInk.com

ISBN: 978-0-9997513-0-5

For V

Can you find these objects?

Abacus, Acorns, Airplane, Alligator, Amethyst, Anchor, Anemone, Angelfish, Ant, Anteater, Apple, Armadillo, Arrow, Artichoke, Asparagus, Avocado, Axe

01000010

Look for these things.

Ballet Slippers, Balloons, Bat, Beach Ball,
Beaver, Beets, Bell, Bicycle, Begonias, Binary Code,
Blackberries, Blueberries, Bluebells, Bluebird, Book,
Boot, Bouquet of Blossoms, Brain, Bubbles, Bull,
Bumblebee, Buttercups, Butterfly

Do you see...

Cabbage, Caged Canary, Cake, Candle, Cat, Celery, Chain, Cheese, Chicken, Clarinet, Clock, Coins, Corn, Cow, Crayons, Crow

Look for these objects.

Dahlia, Daisy, Dandelion, Daffodil, Deer, Dice, DNA,
Dog, Doll, Dolphin, Donkey, Dragonfly, Duck

Do you see these things?

Eagle, Ear, Earth, Eel, Egg, Eggplant, Elephant, Elk, Emerald, Emu, Eye

Can you find...

Falcon, Fan, Ferris Wheel, Fig, Fire, Flamingo, Flute, Footprint, Fork, Four Fifths Fraction, Fox, Foxgloves, Frog, Fruit Salad

Do you see these objects?

Garlic, Gazelle, Gears, Gecko, Geranium, Ginger,
Giraffe, Globe, Goat, Gold, Goldfish, Goose, Gosling,
Grapes, Guitar, Gyroscope

Can you find these things?

Half Note, Hammer, Happy Face, Harp, Heart, Hedgehog, Helicopter, Hibiscus, Hippopotamus, Holly, Honeycomb, Horn, Horse, Hotdog, Hot-Air Balloon, Hourglass

Look for...

Ice Cream, Ice Cubes, Icicles, Idea, Igloo, Iguana, Insects, Iris

Can you find these objects?

Jacks, Jade, Jacket, Jaguar, Jar of Jam, Jasmine, Jasper, Jellyfish, Jellybeans, Jet, Juice, Jupiter

Look for these things.

Kangaroo, Kazoo, Keys, Kestrel, Kite, Kiwi Bird, Kiwi Fruit, Knife, Knitting, Knot, Koala, Kohlrabi, Kumquat

Do you see...

Lace, Ladybug, Lamb, Lamppost, Lavender, Lemons and Limes, Lemur, Lighthouse, Lily, Lion, Llama, Lobster, Lupin

Look for these objects.

Macaroni, Magnet, Magnolia, Mandolin, Mantis, Maple
Leaf, Maracas, Milk, Mitten, Monkey, Moon, Moose,
Mouse, Morning Glory, Morse Code, Moth, Mushrooms

Do you see these things?

Nail, Narwhal, Nautilus, Nectarine, Needle, Neptune, Nest, Neuron, Newt, Nightingale, Noodles, Numbat, Nuts

Can you find...

Ocelot, Octagon, Octopus, Olives, Onions, Orca, Orange, Orangutan, Orchid, Ostrich, Otter, Owl

Do you see these objects?

Paint Palette, Pansy, Peach, Pencil, Penguin, Peony, Piano, Pig, Pineapple, Pinwheel, Polar Bear, Pumpkin, Pushpin, Puzzle

$$ax^2 + bx + c = 0$$

1,000,000,000,000,000

Can you find these things?

Quadratic Equation, Quadrillion, Quail, Quarters, Quarter Note, Quartz, Queen, Queen Anne's Lace, Question Mark, Quill, Quilt, Quince

Look for...

Rabbit, Raccoon, Rain, Rainbow, Raincloud, Raspberries, Rhinoceros, Ribbon, Robot, Rocket, Roller Skate, Rose, Rooster, Ruby Ring

Can you find these objects?

Sailboat, Sandal, Sand Dollar, Scallop Shell, Sea Lion, Seahorse, Seastar, Seaweed, Shark, Skate, Snail, Snowflakes, Snowman, Squid, Stingray, Submarine, Swordfish

Look for these things.

Tent, Thermometer, Thistle, Ticket, Tomato, Traffic Light, Train, Tree, Triangle, Turkey, Tyrannosaurus Rex

Do you see...

Ukulele, Umbrella, Umbrella Plant, Ultramarine, Ultra-Violet, Umber, Underwear, Unequal, Unicycle, Uranus, Urchin, Urn

Look for these objects.

Vanilla Bean and Vanilla Flower, Vapor, Vest, Vine, Vineyard, Violet, Violin, Volcano, Volleyball

Do you see these things?

Wagon, Waffle, Walnuts, Watch, Watermelon, Weasel, Web, Whale, Wheel, Whistle, Wings, Wisteria, Wolf, Woodpecker, Worm, Wrench

Can you find...

X-Chromosome, Xeranthemum Flower, Xerus (African Squirrel), Xylophone, Xyst (Arched Garden Path)

Do you see these objects?

Yacht, Yak, Yardstick, Yarn, Yarrow, Yams, Yellow Light, Yo-yo, Yogurt, Yurt

Can you find these things?

Zebra, Zebra Finch, Zebra Plant, Zebra Swallowtail Butterfly, Zeppelin, Zipper, Zucchini

www.ingramcontent.com/pod-product-compliance
Lightning Source LLC
Chambersburg PA
CBHW050416180526
45159CB00005B/2294